LITTLE PANDA

THE WORLD WELCOMES
HUA MEI
AT THE SAN DIEGO ZOO

JOANNE RYDER

SIMON & SCHUSTER
BOOKS FOR YOUNG READERS
NEW YORK / LONDON / TORONTO / SYDNEY / SINGAPORE

For everyone who loves Hua Mei and wants giant pandas to survive–
especially Jessica, Heather, and Victoria, Cory and Lee, Lucy and Molly

ACKNOWLEDGMENTS

The author is especially grateful to the Research, Animal Care, and Marketing staff at the World-Famous San Diego Zoo for their insight, graciousness, and care in the preparation and review of this manuscript, and thanks them for their kind and thoughtful assistance.

Also, I deeply thank my editor, Jessica Schulte—who first saw the need to tell Hua Mei's story—for her boundless enthusiasm, skill with words, and gentle understanding of the plights of authors and pandas.

The Zoological Society of San Diego would like to acknowledge the support of the following organizations: Zoological Society of San Diego trustees and staff, U.S. Department of the Interior, Consulate General of the People's Republic of China, State Forestry Administration, China Wildlife Conservation Association, Sichuan Forestry Department, China Research and Conservation Center for the Giant Panda, Wolong Nature Reserve, Pacific Bell and the SBC Global Network, as well as all those who continue to support the conservation and research efforts helping to save this critically endangered species.

SIMON & SCHUSTER BOOKS FOR YOUNG READERS

 An imprint of Simon & Schuster Children's Publishing Division

1230 Avenue of the Americas, New York, New York 10020

Book design by Heather Wood. The text of this book is set in Meta Book.

Printed and bound in the United States of America

ISBN 0-689-84310-0 / LC# 00-111905

A minimum of 5% hardcover and 4% paperback of the net retail proceeds will go to
worldwide giant panda conservation efforts of the World-Famous San Diego Zoo.

Hua Mei™ and World-Famous San Diego Zoo® are trademarks of the Zoological Society of San Diego. Used with permission.

For more information about giant pandas, please contact

Pacific Bell Giant Panda Research Center

San Diego Zoo

P.O. Box 551

San Diego, CA 92112-0551

Or visit the Web site at www.SanDiegoZoo.org

There she goes—
climbing with wobbly legs,
up and up and up and up.

*Pandas are natural climbers. They use their
stronger front legs to pull themselves as they climb.*

Whoops!
She flips
upside down.

Whee!
She sits
rightside up.

A little panda finds treasure everywhere.
Just the right size, a stick becomes a toy
Hua Mei bites, tastes, and juggles in her paws.

*Keepers and scientists scatter items
for the pandas to discover: sometimes
a burlap bag, sometimes a mound of
sawdust to roll in, and sometimes a
"bamboosicle"—a hollow bamboo reed
filled with tasty treats to snack on.*

A tiny acrobat scrambles
in her very own playground.

Hua Mei pulls and climbs,
testing the branches,
testing her own strength.

Hua Mei loves to have her head and back gently scratched. (Her fur feels much like a German shepherd's.)
If she comes when the keepers call her, Hua Mei is rewarded with lots of scratching! Keepers need to
be able to depend on Hua Mei coming when called so that checkups and doctor visits are easy for everyone.

Hua Mei wanders,
drawn to the
sparkling pool,
patting the water,
dipping into coolness.

A young panda
makes her own discoveries
while her mama, Bai Yun
(pronounced *By Yoon*),
feasts on bamboo.

Observers are specially trained people who take notes about the things pandas do all day. When the pandas are active—eating and climbing and playing—the observers are very busy writing about what the animals do.

Pandas are known as bamboo bears because they eat up to forty pounds of bamboo a day. Their diet changes with the seasons. Sometimes they eat only the leaves and other times they chew on just the thick, woody stems.

Bai Yun grasps bamboo with nimble paws. With her strong teeth, she crushes stems, ripping and stripping slender leaves.

Soon Hua Mei will have all her teeth.
Then she will be a bamboo bear like her mama,
big enough to eat the tall, tall grass.

But for now, when she's hungry,
Hua Mei cuddles close to her mama,
nursing, sipping warm, rich milk.

Hua Mei
looks up
a leafy tower.
Wishing
herself high,
she starts
to climb.

*Little pandas have
sharp claws to help
them climb trees.
A mother panda
doesn't worry when
her baby climbs up
high. Pandas are
safer in the branches
of a tree than on the
ground where they
can be hurt by
other animals.*

She peeks through branches
at the world below,
at her mama never very far away.

Hua Mei
tags her mama—
catch me if you can—
and runs away.

*Bai Yun weighs about 200 pounds.
She knows she must be gentle when she
plays with little Hua Mei, who weighs
only about 20 pounds in these photos.*

Playful pandas roll and tumble making up a game all their own.

Chirping softly, she feels her mama's big arms scooping her up, wrapping around her, catching her with a hug.

One year old, Hua Mei
is a promise come true—
a lively, healthy giant panda.

Hua Mei will stay with her mother for about 18 months and then will live by herself. In nature, giant pandas live alone. They come together only to mate. Fewer than 1,000 giant pandas survive in the world today. It is important to protect these rare animals from extinction.

May she
and all pandas
live long,
be well, be safe
on our good earth.